Follow this link to claim your free gift

https://deborah-smith.net/roadmapgift/

Online Coach:
Read Learn Perform

Contact:
www.deborah-smith.net

Facebook Page:
Lees Leer Presteer Read Learn Perform

Dr Deborah J Smith **coahces**
teachers and parents.

READ LEARN PERFORM

She achieved her PhD in Education:
Curriculum and Instructional
Development and Design.
She also achieved the following degrees:
M.Ed. Educational
Guidance and Counselling
B.Ed. (hons.) Remedial Teaching
B.Ed. (hons.) Educational Psychology

Printed and distributed by:
Dr Deborah J Smith
Pretoria, South Africa

Every topic in this book is designed to provide essential skills towards achieving a desired outcome in a specific order.

GLOBAL POSITION IN STRUCTURE (GPS)

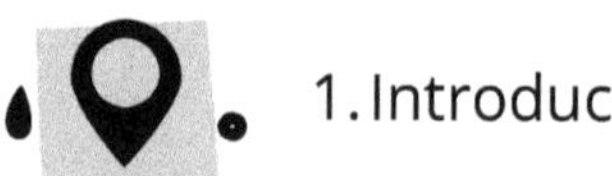
1. Introduction

2. Auditory skills

3. Visual skills

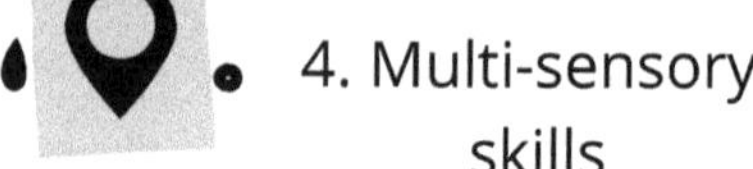
4. Multi-sensory skills

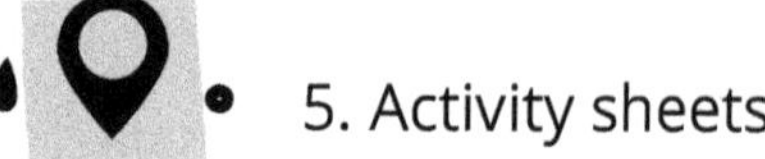
5. Activity sheets

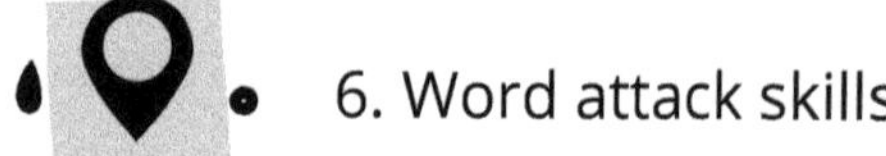
6. Word attack skills

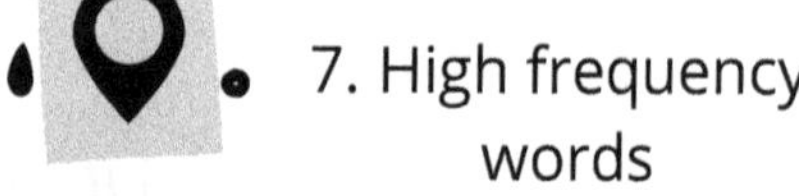
7. High frequency words

8. Comprehension

Every topic in this book is designed to provide essential skills towards achieving a <u>desired outcome</u> in a <u>specific order</u>.

GLOBAL POSITION IN STRUCTURE (GPS)

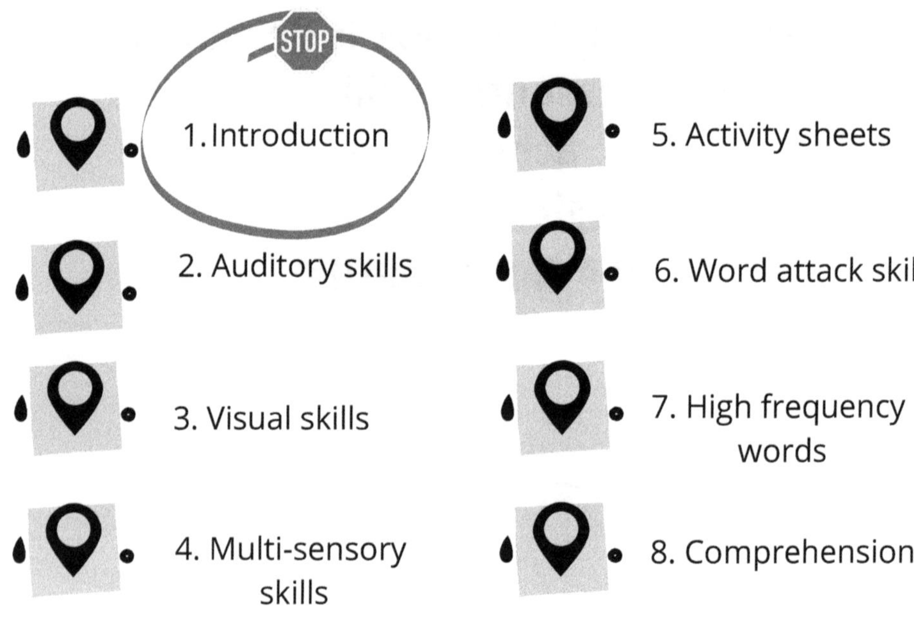

1. Introduction

- When do the **scribbles** on the page turn into words that learners can **understand**?
- When does reading become **reading**?
- Learners must be instructed **systematically** and with clear **goals** in mind throughout the process of reading with understanding.

This programme will demonstrate the systematic and goal-oriented steps of teaching reading in a practical manner.

Reading **with understanding** is one of the most complex internal processes. Therefore, we must **simplify** the reading process, so that it can be unpacked and taught.

The **Simple View of Reading** (Stuart et al. 2008: 5) is used to explain how **decoding** skills should always occur simultaneously and integrated with **reading comprehension.**

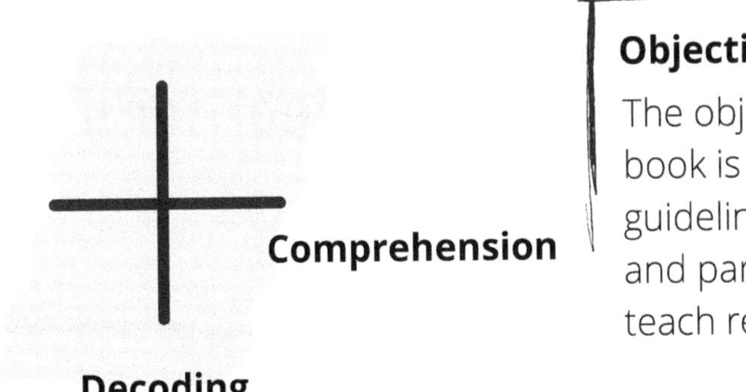

Objective

The objective of this book is to provide guidelines to teachers and parents to teach reading effectively.

IMPORTANT NOTE

The teaching of reading ought to be systematic, with a specific objective in mind.

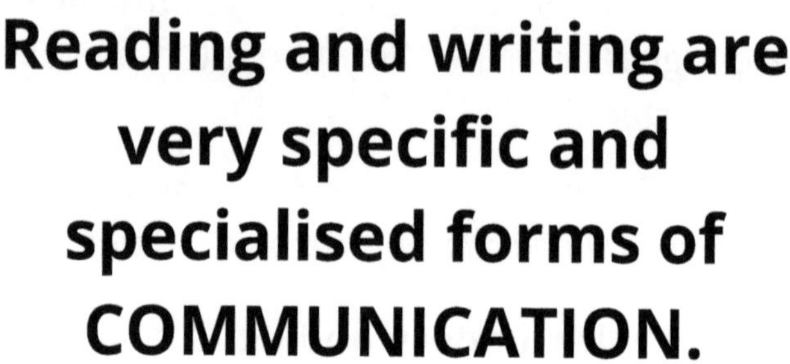

Reading and writing are very specific and specialised forms of COMMUNICATION.

The structure of each learner's brain is unique.

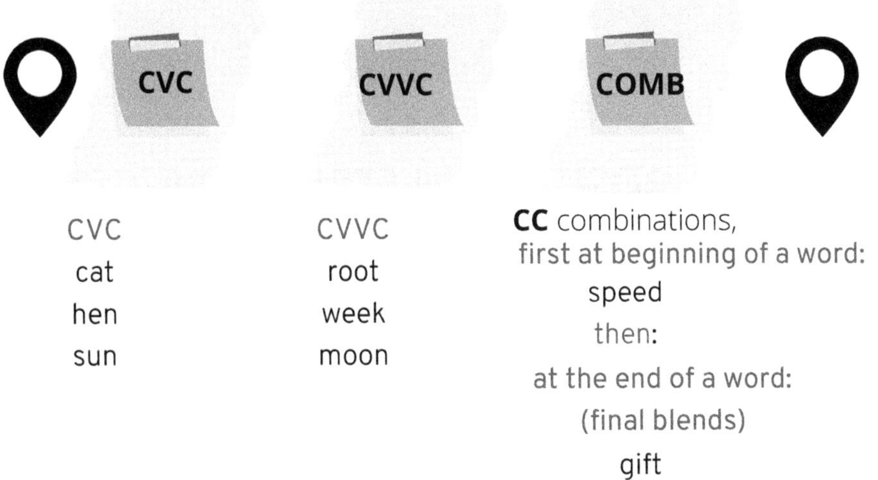

Expose systematically and allow ample time for exercise.

Beginner readers start reading words as explained in the abovementioned – first the high frequency words **CVC** where **C** means consonant and **V** means vowel – words such as **cat**, **hen**, **sit**. Once learners have learnt to read a variety of **CVC** words, they move onto reading digraphs (two letters that make up one sound). They will learn the sounds /**ch**/ and /**sh**/ and be shown how to represent these sounds as letters, words such as **ship**, **shop**, **chip, chat** *(word families).*

Thereafter you can introduce **high frequency words** in pattern **CVVC**, words such as **root**, **week**, **weak**. The consonant blends are only introduced once the combinations of **CVC** and **CVVC** are well practised.

First start with the blends at the **begining** of a word in the pattern of **CCVVC** such as **speed**, **spoon**, and then **final blends** (consonant blends **CVCC** at the end of a word) such as **gift**, **hand**, **fast**.

Enough time must be provided for each section as indicated above. Pictures or illustrations can be used very succesfully when teaching a sound, but be careful when using pictures to teach words. Learners tend to recognise the illustration and not decode the word.

The use of illustrations will be discussed in more detail later.

GLOBAL POSITION IN STRUCTURE (GPS)

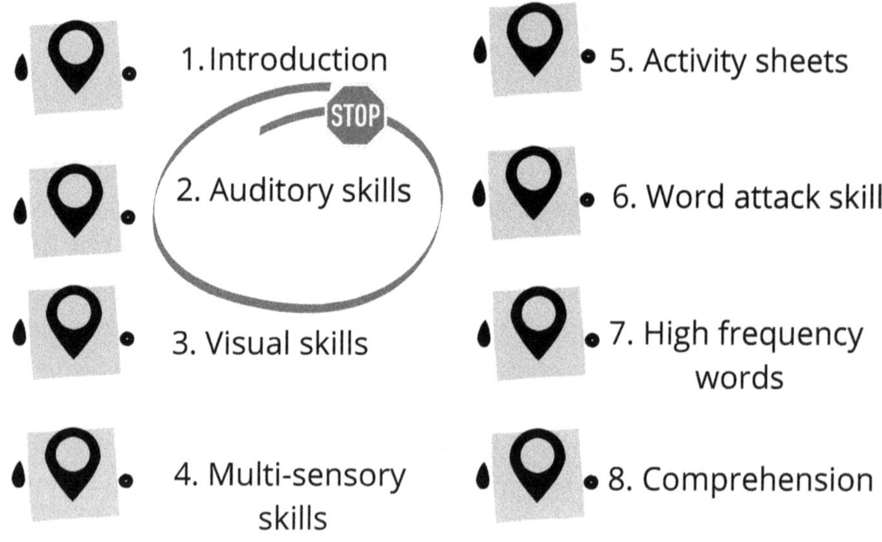

2.1 Auditory skills ••• information

As auditory skills are not visibly obvious,
we tend to oversee the importance thereof.

Auditory skills cannot be compared to the ability to hear.

Learners' ability to hear might be rightfully in place and very effective, but their perceptual abilities might be problematic.

There is an assumption that reading is primarily visual **BUT it is not!**

Research has proved that **auditory skills** result in more successful reading than visual perceptual skills.

A very elementary definition of auditory perceptual skills is:

Auditory perception refers to the ability of the brain to interpret and create a clear impression of sounds.

A learner must first hear the sound before they can assign a letter to the sound.
Auditory skills form an important building block for reading and learning.

2.2 Auditory skills  games

- Where do you **hear** the sound in the word:
  Example: where do you hear the sound **s** in the word: **rats**.

- **Rhymes**...
  Teach the learners rhymes and clap to the rhythm of the rhyme.

- **Search** for items (amongst others) that start or end with a specific sound. Physical items or pictures/illustrations could be used.
  Example: find a picture that starts with a **s** sound: **sun**, **swim**, **sit.**
  Find an item that ends with a **m** sound: **drum**, **dam**

- **Telephone**...
  Let the learners sit in a circle. Start by whispering a short message to the child closest to you. Each one should whisper the same message to the next learner. Let the last one repeat the message that was heard. This is a fun game and learners love playing it.

- **Follow instructions...**
  Play "Master chef". Use empty containers or bottles. Assign an ingredient to a coloured box for example: the red box is flour, the yellow box is sugar, the brown box is salt.
  Give **oral** instructions to bake a cake, for example: Add 2 sugars in the bowl, add 5 flours and 3 salts etc.
  Learners can take turns to give instructions to fellow students. This game can be adapted to suit the learners' own interests.

2.2 Auditory skills  games

- **Tongue teasers**...

  She sells seashells by the seashore,
  The shells she sells are seashells, I'm sure.
  So if she sells seashells on the seashore,
  Then I'm sure she sells seashore shells....etc.

- **Simon says...**

- **Lister to sounds in the environment**

  Listen to sounds in the environment and try to identify them. Also, prompt the learner to construct a sentence using the identified objects.

2.3 Auditory skills in the reading lesson

Herewith an example of the manner in which auditory skills is presented in a reading lesson:
Listen to the word: **bag**
Which **sounds** do you hear?

Learners could transfer beans, buttons or marbles from one container to another for each sound they hear for example, a button for each sound.

Learners listen to short sentences, and have to repeat the sentences word by word, i.e. the lady washed the pot

Is the word **day** in the word **yesterday**?
Is the word **yes** in the word **yesterday**?
Is the word **night** in the word **yesterday**?
Is the word **Saturday** in the word **yesterday**?
When was **yesterday**?
Use **yesterday** in a sentence.
What does the word **night** mean?
Use **night** in a sentence.

Listen to the following words. You have to say if the words differ or are the same:
rot / rat
pear / bear
yoke / joke

2.3 Auditory skills in the reading lesson

Say the next word: **bear**
Remove the **b** and replace it with a **f**
What is it now?
Yes, it is **fear**.
Have you ever had a **fear** of something?
Are you scared when you have **fear** of something?
Pronounce the word **fear**.
Replace the **f** with a **d**
Which word is it now?
Yes, it is the word **dear**.
Have you ever been called my **dear**?
Remove the **r** from the word **dear** and replace it with a **d**.
Which word do you have now? It is the word **dead**.
A plant could be **dead**, or an animal could be **dead**.
Remove the two **d** from the word and add a **t** at the end.
Which word is it now? It is the word **eat**. What did you **eat** this morning?

Learners must first hear the sound before they are able to write the sound

2.4 Auditory skills

NB road signs

- It is of utmost importance that learners are able to **hear** and **identify** the sounds. One should furthermore, ensure that learners understand that the **meaning of words alter** when a specific sound is either **added** or **omitted** or **altered**.

Teach the meaning of the words explicitly.

- The addition or omision of sounds changes the meaning of words.

- Prior knowledge of learners should always be linked to new sounds and word meanings.

ALWAYS READ WITH COMPREHENSION FOR COMPREHENSION.

2.5 Auditory skills reading difficulties

The following can serve as an indication of problematic auditory perceptual skills when reading:

- **Auditory discrimination problems**: The ability to notice, compare, and distinguish between the distinct and separate sounds in words. Learners find it difficult to distinguish between sounds that are similar for example: **pack** vs. **back**. These might be the cause that learners are unable to follow directions even when the they appear to be paying attention.

- **Auditory figure-ground discrimination**: Learners must be able to identify sounds against a noisy background. They might struggle to identify a sound between others, for example, where do you hear the sound **t** in the word **cat**?

- **Auditory sequencing:** The ability to understand and recall the order of sounds and words. Learners might struggle to make sense of a word or sentence which they did not hear in the entirety. Comprehension will be problematic and they do not understand the storyline.

2.5 Auditory skills reading difficulties

- **Auditory closure:** The ability to complete or add sounds which were not heard, in order to understand what was heard. For example, when the teacher speaks to the child and a bus goes by, he might only hear **"Go and fe ... your pe..."** and needs auditory closure to understand that the teacher meant **"Go and fetch your pen."**

- **Auditory analysis and auditory synthesis:**

  Auditory analysis: is the ability to divide words into syllables (and also the ability to divide sentences into words), i.e. **butterfly** = **but** + **ter** + **fly**.

  Auditory synthesis: refers to the ability to put sounds or words together to make a new word or sentence, i.e. **b** + **a** + **t** = **bat**.

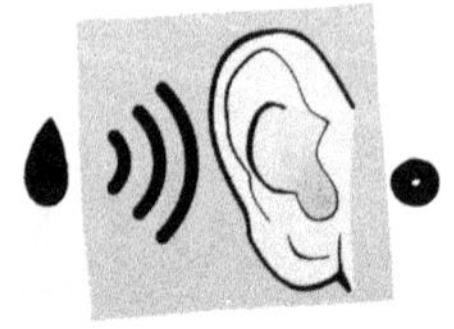

GLOBAL POSITION IN STRUCTURE (GPS)

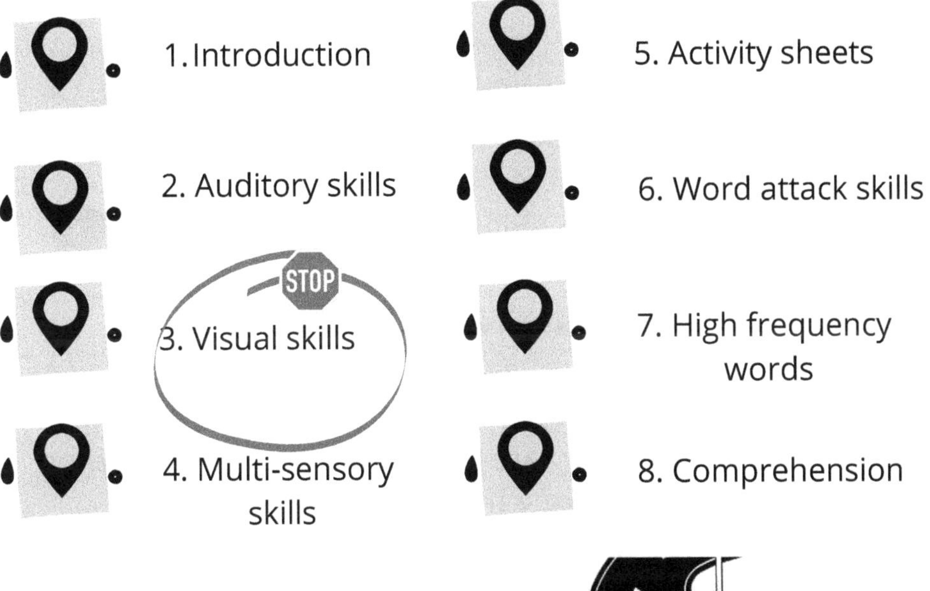

3.1 Visual skills information

Foundation phase learners depend largely on the movement and experience of the letter/sound on their own bodies.

We will first write it in the **air**, **sand** or with chalk on the **pavement** in **BIG LARGE movements.**

Definition:
The term **visual perceptual skills** refers to the ability of the **brain** to structure to meaning, **make sense of what is seen**.

It is not the ability of the eyes to see.

Learners between the ages of **4 and 7** are in the i**ntuitive phase**, therefore they **act** intuitively on perception **rather than thinking** before acting.

3.1 Visual skills information

The critical development of **position in space** orientation happens between the **ages of 7 and 9.**

We expect learners to read, write and copy from another source at this age. Keep in mind that this ability is still being developed in the foundation phase. Obviously they are still making mistakes, thus **have mercy**!

•••••••••••••••••••

Association:
Research has proved that **associations** (embedded mnemonics) greatly supports the recognition of letters and improves learning. Various studies *(Ehri, 2014; Ehri, Deffner, & Wilce, 1984; McNamara, 2012; Schmidman & Ehri, 2010)* have proved that such embedded mnemonic pictures can **reduce** the amounts of **repetition** needed for kids to learn the letters and sounds. Implementing this strategy will also cause **less confusion**, better **long-term memory,** and greater ability to **transfer or apply** this knowledge in reading and spelling.

This technique **SHOULD NOT** be used for the **learning of high frequency words**.
(Ehri, 2014; Ehri, Deffner &Wilce, 1984; McNamara, 2021; Schmidman & Ehri, 2010)

Art Credit: The example of a visual mnemonic for teaching decoding was provided by the artist Cat MacInnes, from www.spelfabet.com.au/materials"

3.2 Visual skills games

- Obstacle Course
- Building with blocks
- I spy with my tiny tiny eye...
- Jungle gym
- Maze games
- Sit **on** the ball,
  behind the ball
  next to the ball...

Match the pictures
Domino cards
Colouring pages
Find Wally in the picture
Paint in different colours

Tidy and neat
Keep the classroom organised and tidy as learners who experience problematic functioning of visual skills will not be able to find items in an untidy room.

Puzzles
Puzzles are great for stimulating visual skills. Should there be no puzzles, make your own drawings and colour them, or cut images from magazines into smaller pieces.

Memory games
Show a range of objects/pictures to learners, then cover them. Ask the learners to unpack or name them in the correct sequence.

3.3 Visual skills in the reading lesson

Look at the first letter. Find it between the others.

b b d d p q p b d

Complete the rhyme:
The cat on the ...

Always bring the background knowledge and understanding of learners to the reading lesson by asking related questions.

Complete the word:
Ca...

Learners might guess the word **cat**.
Teacher asks: "Have you ever touched a **cat**?"
What are the colours you've seen a **cat** in?
What is the difference between a **cat** as a pet and a **cat-scan**?

Look at the first picture, which one is different...

Colour the apple red.

3.3 Visual skills in the reading lesson

- **What will happen next...**

- Look for the following word: **bed**

met bed led fed bed

The man sat on the bed.

The hen sat on a bed of feathers.

Always bring the learners' prior knowledge to the lesson by means of questions.

3.4 Visual skills

NB road signs

- It is of utmost importanct that learners are able to **hear** the sound and identify and distinguish between them. They are only ready to learn to write them once they are able to successfully hear and identify the sounds.

- Start with familiar/ known sounds.

- Always integrate prior knowledge and comprehension when teaching reading. Use a variety of questions during the teaching of reading to establish comprehension and to link prior knowledge to the lesson.

- Use colour, also allow learners to use colour.

3.5 Visual skills reading difficulties

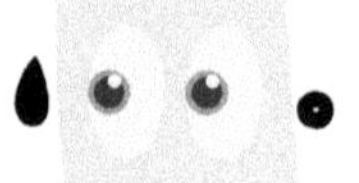

The following serve as an indication of **problematic** visual perceptual skills when reading:

- **Visual analysis and synthesis**
  Learners are not able to distinguish/analyse a unit from the whole. Learners that experiece difficulty in this area find it difficult to identify and distinguish between the individual sounds in a word. They are also required to assemble a whole from the units. These learners find it difficult to build puzzles as well as other activities such as onset and rime.

- **Visual discrimination**
  The ability to pay attention to detail and to correctly perceive letters and numbers where there is only a small difference between them for example **S** and **5**, **m, n** and **u** as well as **k,h**

- **Visual figure-ground**
  Figure-ground perception helps learners **find** the **correct** information against a **busy background**. Learners that find this difficult might lose their place when reading or copying from the black board.

3.5 Visual skills reading difficulties

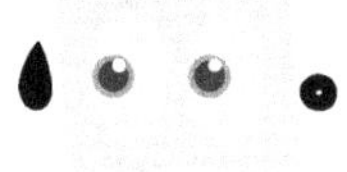

Visual Memory and Visual Sequential Memory

Visual memory is necessary to **remember** sightwords whereas visual **sequential memory** helps to remember the order of the letters. Learners that experience problems with these visual perceptual skills might be weak at spelling and might struggle to remember the sightwords, for example sequence of letters in words like board and broad.

Visual Closure

Visual closure skills can help the learner to make sense of things that are only **partly** visible.

Learners that struggle with visual closure might not be able to read fluently or decode words accurately or complete the outstanding letters in words or sentences.

Visual Form Constancy

The ability to distinguish one object from another similar object such as being able to tell the difference between the letter **b** and **d** or **3** and **8**. Though the forms are similar in shape, they are very different in meaning.

GLOBAL POSITION IN STRUCTURE (GPS)

1. Introduction

2. Auditory skills

3. Visual skills

4. Multi-sensory skills

5. Activity sheets

6. Word attack skills

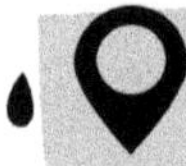
7. High frequency words

8. Comprehension

STOP

After 2 weeks we remember:

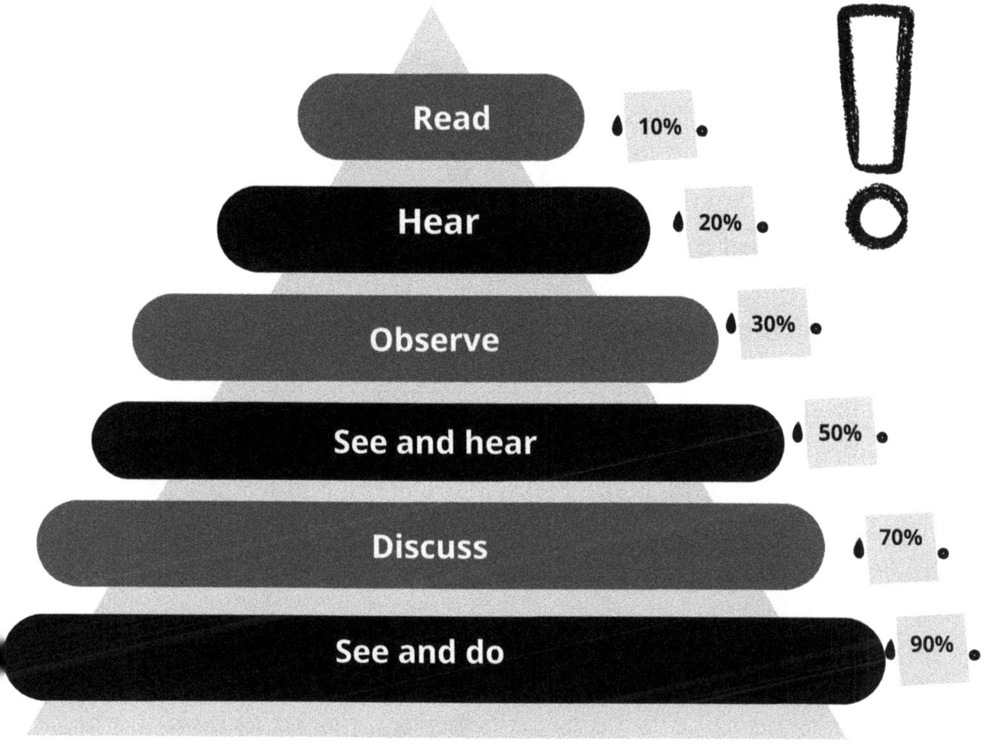

Read 10%

Hear 20%

Observe 30%

See and hear 50%

Discuss 70%

See and do 90%

(Edgar Dale 1969)

4.2 Multi-sensory skills games

A multi-sensory skill approach means that the learning would happen **more effectively** should there be **more than one** sensory stimulation during learning and reading.

For more information, consult Edgar Dale's "Cone of experience".

- Build the letters with **clay**.
- Make **mud cakes**.
- Glue **coloured sand**.
- Create a **sensory garden**.
- Use 4 or 5 containers each with different items of different **textures** inside. Blindfold the learners and let them explore and interact with one of the textures. They should now attempt to describe the texture.
- Paint with **balloons**..
- Mix Maizena and water to a **paste**. Let the learners use their fingers to write and draw figures in the paste. The figure will remain for a while but will disappear shortly. The younger ones will enjoy this!

- **Treasure hunt** in the sand: Hide a few small toys in the sand and let the learners search for them.

Rice and Ice game: Mix cooked rice and coloured ice cubes in the same bowl. Let the learners explore the textures. They will also see how the rice changes colour.

4.3 Multi-sensory skills in the reading lesson

Show the word.
The word could also be on the **theme** table.
Say the word out loud.
Put a **pebble** in a glass for every sound you **hear**.
Close your eyes.
Try to see the word **in your mind**.
Show the word.
What is the **meaning** of the word?
Write the word in **sand** or on paper (rather sand as it could be overwritten if wrong, remember we are learning and it is a **process**).

- Hopscotch sightword or high frequency words.
- Focus on the letter-sound : a pebble for each identified sound. After this the learners will be able to write the word.

Read it.
Build it.
Write it.

4.4 Multi-sensory skills

NB road signs

- Focus on the individual sounds.

- Make use of more than one sense to teach the learners.

- See the sounds.
  Say the sounds.
  Write the sounds.
  Give a meaning to the word.

- Read more about Orton-Gillingham activities

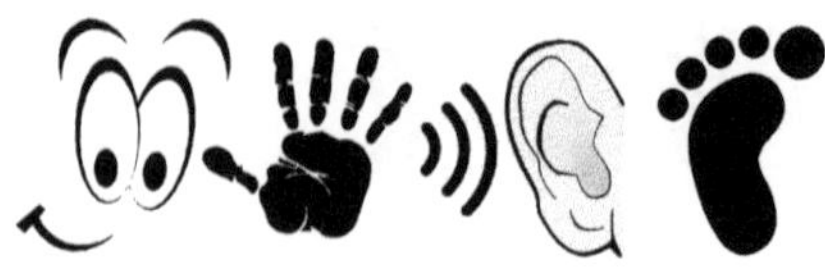

GLOBAL POSITION IN STRUCTURE (GPS)

1. Introduction
2. Auditory skills
3. Visual skills
4. Multi-sensory skills

5. Activity sheets
6. Word attack skills

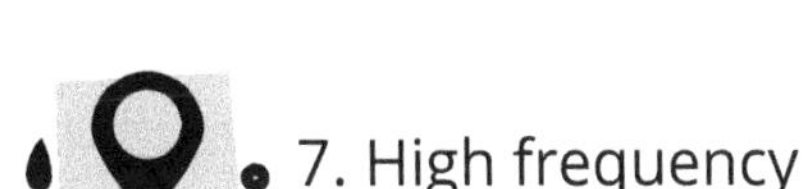

7. High frequency words

8. Comprehension

5.1 Activity sheets

information

- Activity sheets can only be introduced once the learners are able to hear the sounds and identify them correctly. Activity sheets can solely be implemented to establish and ground the teaching that has already occured.

- Do not use activity sheets to teach reading.

- Illustrations can be used to teach sounds but be careful to use illustrations to teach the spelling of words.

- Careful select a range of activity sheets to ensure that different cognitive skills are stimulated.

5.2 Activity sheets illustrations

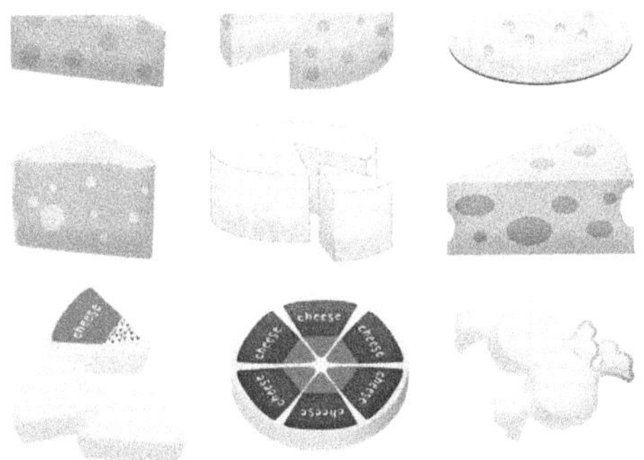

This compound picture is **not** a good example to illustrate the word 'cheese'. The variety of different kinds or shapes of cheese might confuse the learners.

This picture is not good example to illustrate the word 'cheese', as the mouse may divert attention.

This unambiguous picture serves as a good example.

5.3 Activity sheets instructions

Use a variety of activity sheets to excercise and establish the same concept, sound or word.

Identify the sound
(two adjacent words)
bare bear
Use unambiguous
illustrations

Identify amongst **similar words**
mouse, moose, house,

Complete the sentence...
The man sees the

____

(use unambiguous illustration)

GLOBAL POSITION IN STRUCTURE (GPS)

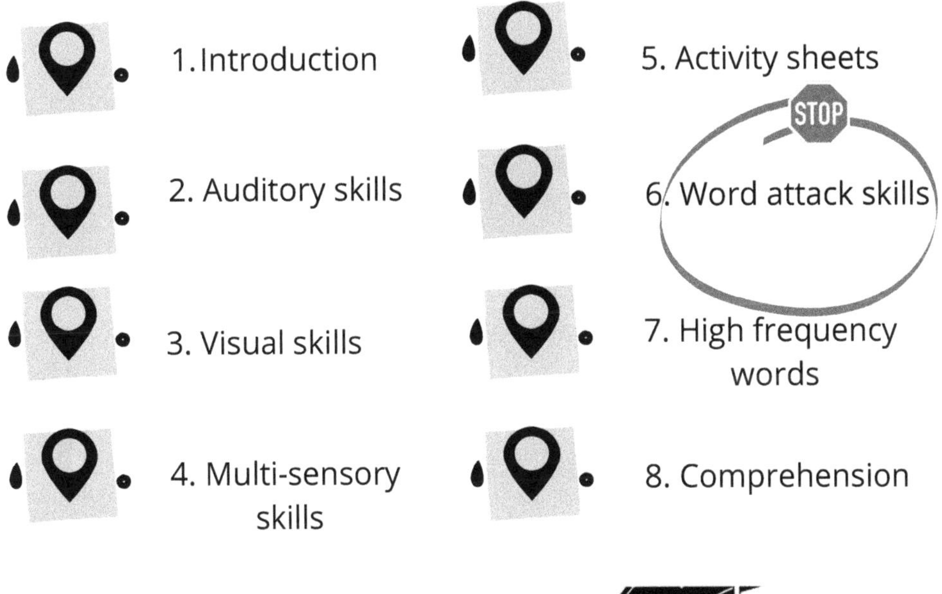

6.1 Word attack skills information

What is word attack skills?

Word attack skills help learners **decode** unfamiliar words. This strategy enables learners to strategically **analyse** words and **find meaning**. Word attack strategies help students **decode, pronounce or understand** unfamiliar words when reading.

Word attack skills assist learners to identify **patterns** in words. Learners should use a **variety** of these strategies when reading. If one strategy does not help to decode the word, they should **try another strategy.**

Learners must be able to **infer** word meaning by using **suffixes** for an example. This forms a crucial skill for reading comprehension.

Learners should realise that the addition or omitting of sounds can change the meaning of words.

6.2 Word attack skills information

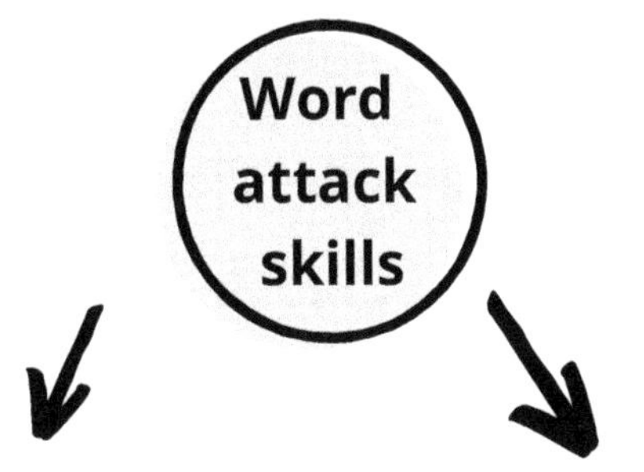

Rhyme

Rhyme teaches learners about the **language, word families, contribute to the rythm and stimulate vocabulary** development. Learners learn to listen closely for sounds within words.

Onset and rime

Helps learners to recognize common 'chunks' within words. This can help students decode new words when reading and spelling words when writing. Improve phonological awareness by helping learners learn about **word families. Phonetical awareness** is an essential skill used to **hear sounds, syllables, and words** in speech

The **onset** is the initial phonological unit of any word.

Rime refers to the string of letters that follow, usually a vowel and final consonants.

In the word **pen**
·**p** is the onset
·**en** is the rime

In the word **twig**
·**tw** is the onset
·**ig** is the rime

•6.3 Word attack skills

examples

- **Word attack skills** serve as an **umbrella** term of skills learners need to **decode** difficult or unfamiliar words.

- **Picture books**
  Pictures books are designed in a specific way to demonstrate the text. This involves the context clues and expectancy of words and concepts.
  Are there characters or objects or specific actions that can assist to interpret the illustration ?

- **Visual attack**
  Use visual characteristics of a word to determine the meaning for example the identfication of known parts within the word, using syllables, prefixes, suffixes and root words.

- **Use prior knowledge**
  Ask learners what they know about the subject/concept at hand. Try to make connections between the known information and the new concept. Prompt learners to provide a word that will relate to the text.

GLOBAL POSITION IN STRUCTURE (GPS)

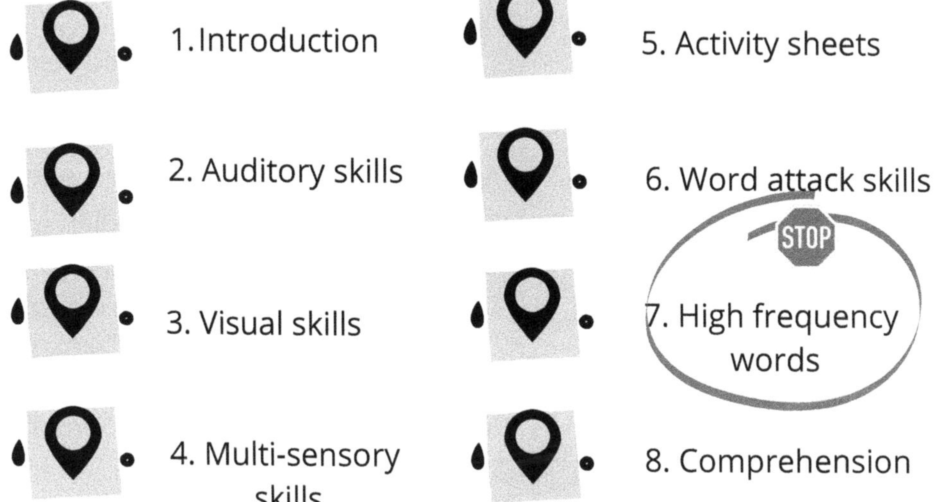

7.1 High frequency words

What are high frequency words?

High frequency words are those words which occur most frequently in written material.

Why are high frequency words important?

High frequency words are words that are immediately recognized as a whole and do not require word analysis for identification thus supporting reading fluency and comprehension of a text.

Games can successfully be incorporated to teach high frequency words

Research proved : (Hayes C, 2013)

7.2 High frequency words

games

Card games like **Snap** and **Bingo** can be used very succesfully to teach and practise high frequency words.

Each learner receives a card with high frequency words. Teacher calls out a random word from the list. Learners circle or cross the words on their worksheets. First one to complete a row shouts; **Bingo**

Flash cards
Snap
Automation of words

7.2 High frequency words games

Lists
Learners indicate
which words they are able to read.

here	☑	☐
those	☐	☒
because	☑	☐
want	☐	☒
have	☑	☐

Write the same words using different colours

had them came soon then

had them came soon then

had them came soon then

had them came soon then

Learners may play against time **ONLY** when they are comfortable to reading the words. Use these games to **practise the words NOT to teach new words.** Also, some learners struggle to perform under pressure. Do not use this strategy if that might be the case.

GLOBAL POSITION IN STRUCTURE (GPS)

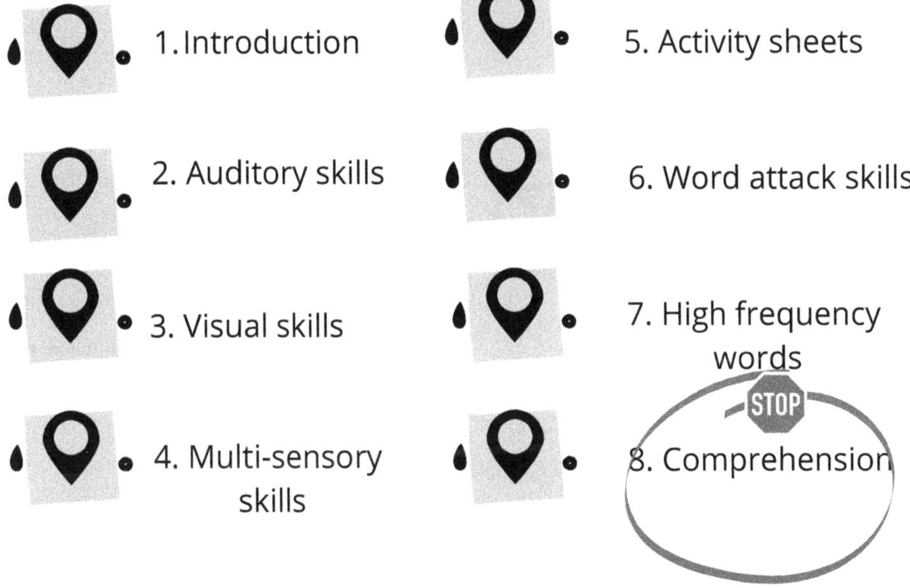

8.1 Comprehension information

The ultimate **goal** of reading is to **read with comprehension**.

80% of learning has already occurred once learners are able to read with understanding.

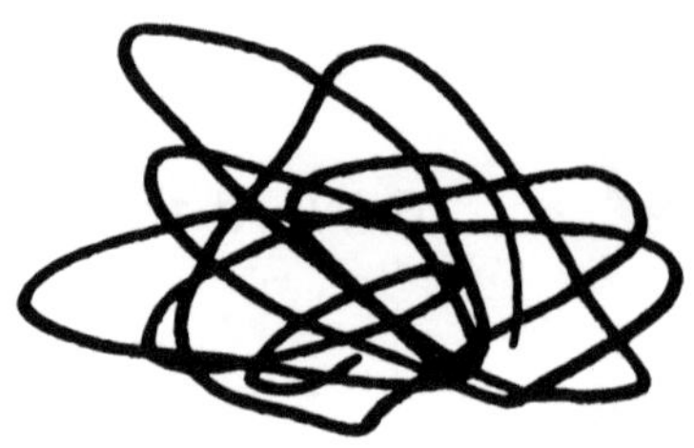

Foundation phase learners must understand that the scribbles on paper have meaning.

The reading passage should always be available to the readers when assessing reading comprehension as the focus is on **comprehension** and not **memory**.

Reading comprehension is not ONLY retrieving direct explicit information from a text.

8.1 Comprehension information

Academic vocabulary should be taught to learners directly .

Explain the **meaning** of the vocabulary that is used for instruction, such as **Explain** or **Compare** or **Name**.
Also **demonstrate** how to answer questions especially the **double-barrelled quesions** such as:
"List two reasons why Johnny was heartbroken. What is your opinion?"

Vocabulary	Vocabulary including the extension thereof is the most important strategy to teach reading comprehension. Not only new difficult words, but also academic words such as **Illustrate** or **Explain** or **Compare** should be addressed.
Prior knowledge	Prior knowledge : Foundation phase learners must always **integrate new knowledge to that which is known to them**. This is a contructive and on-going process.
Meta-cognitive skills	Meta cognitive skills : Those skills necessary to gain understanding in the '**problem-for-me**' situation. This includes the ability to make inferences, conclude, evaluate text but also the ability to '**read between the lines**' and appreciate the author's stance.

8.2 Comprehension 

example

Marked text can be succesfully incorporated in the teaching of reading comprehension strategies. Learners will not see the marked text. Teachers mark the text whilst preparing for the lesson. The words that you select should be very specific, either for teaching vocabulary, to stimulate meta cognitive skills or to apply prior learning to improve the learning experience.

Example:

"Hippos are vegetarians. They eat grass."

"It's not what they eat, Erdvark, it is what they do. When they are annoyed, they trample everything. It's a fact! If we mess with them, we'll end up flat banana skins. Besides-"

Erdvark shook his ears. "I don't want to hear that boring old story of how hippos are resonsible for more deaths in Africa than any other animal –"

"But it's a fact!"

"Well, exactly. But only if you get in their way, Pangolin. And I don't plan to get in a hippo's way. I don't plan to end up like an old banana skin. My only plan is to stroll down to the river where it's cool and gobble up plenty of dragonflies.

(Hotel Pangolin p 65, Hofmeyr)

8.2 Comprehension

example

Use these markers to implement the comprehension strategies as explained.

- What is a vegetarian? What does 'n vetgetarian eat?
- Who is the vegetarian in this text?
- Why does the author refer to 'flat banana skin"?
- Have you seen a 'flat banana skin"?
- Does this word mean that a dragon can fly?
- Do they also want to trample on dragonflies?

Drawing

A strategy that is very successful in the foundation phase is the use of **DRAWINGS**.

Request learners to draw a picture of the story as you read it aloud. Read **slowly,** allowing learners enough time to gain understanding of the text. These illustrations might not be in the likes of a Van Gogh, but they will and must be able to explain the drawings.

Using the same text as on the previous page, **ask learners to draw an annoyed hippo's face.**

You will be able to see if the learners understood that a hippo gets annoyed only when disturbed. Their illustration should include something or someone that irritates or annoyes the hippo.

This is an example of what a 10 year old did. It was done during a History lesson as part of an autobiography of Michael Angelo. Michael Angelo is busy sculpting the Maria sculpture.

8.2 Comprehension example

Request learners to compile their own questions and submit answers.

One of the most important aspects of teaching reading successfully is to ensure that learners should **ENJOY** reading.

Foundation phase learners enjoy imaginary play, especially **fantasy-playing teacher-teacher**!

Create the opportunity for them to structure their **own questions AND to pose the question to fellow learners**. They have to verify the answers themselves. This must be an oral activity so that the teacher can monitor the comprehension levels of the learners.

This is a fun activity and should rightfully be so. It also stimulates new reading comprehension strategies such as:

- Internalising information
- Meta-cognitive skills such as synthesis, analysis and evaluation.

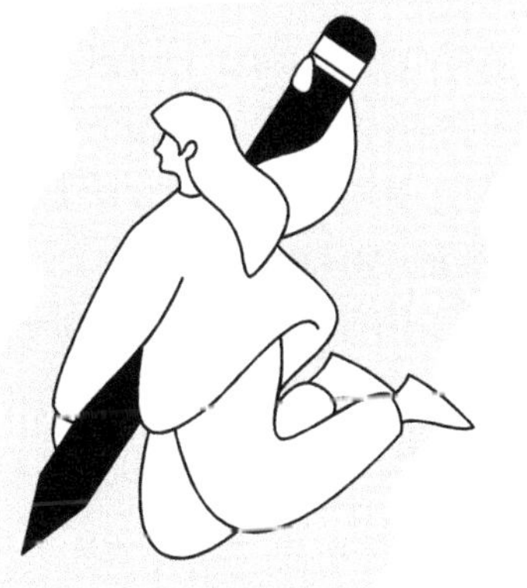

References 

•Ehri, L.C. (2014) Orthographic Mapping in the Acquisition of Sight Word Reading, Spelling Memory, and Vocabulary Learning, Scientific Studies of Reading, 18:1, 5-21, DOI: 10.1080/10888438.2013.819356

•Ehri, L. C., Deffner, N. D., & Wilce, L. S. (1984). Pictorial mnemonics for phonics. Journal of Educational Psychology, 76(5), 880–893. https://doi.org/10.1037/0022-0663.76.5.880

•Department of Education and Early Childhood Development and the Melbourne Institute of Applied Economic and Social Research. Read to young children May 2013

•Harber, Jean R. Are Perceptual Skills Necessary for Success in Reading? Which Ones? Reading Horizons: A Journal of Literacy and Language Arts

•Hayes, Colleen. May 2016. The Effects of Sight Word Instruction on Students' Reading Abilities St. John Fisher Collage

•Hedda Meadan, Julia B. Stoner, Howard P. Fall 2008. Word Recognition Among Young Children At-Risk

•Hofmeyr, D. 2021. Hotel Pangolin. CTP Printers. Cape Town.

•Picture-Supported vs. Word-Only. Illinois State University., Assistive Technology Outcomes and Benefits. Vol.5, Num. 1

•Kraus, Nina PhD; Anderson, Samira AuD, PhD. The Hearing Journal: September 2013 - Volume 66 - Issue 9 –p40

•McNamara, G. (2012). The effectiveness of embedded picture mnemonic alphabet cards on letter recognition and letter sound knowledge. Unpublished Master's thesis, Rowan University.

•Shmidman, A., & Ehri, L. (2010) Embedded picture mnemonics to learn letters. Scientific Studies of Reading, 14:2, 159-182, DOI: 10.1080/10888430903117492

Follow this link to claim your free gift

https://deborah-smith.net/roadmapgift/

www.ingramcontent.com/pod-product-compliance
Ingram Content Group UK Ltd.
Pitfield, Milton Keynes, MK11 3LW, UK
UKHW020421250726
13967UKWH00007B/2760

9 781998 950836